PIANO ✴ VOCAL ✴ GUITAR

Frank SINATRA
CHRISTMAS COLLECTION

T0079942

ISBN 978-1-4234-6353-5

HAL•LEONARD®
CORPORATION
7777 W. BLUEMOUND RD. P.O. BOX 13819 MILWAUKEE, WI 53213

Visit Hal Leonard Online at
www.halleonard.com

CHRISTMAS MEM'RIES

Words by ALAN and MARILYN BERGMAN
Music by DON COSTA

Sing-ing car-ols, string-ing pop-corn, mak-ing foot-prints in the snow; mem-'ries, Christ-mas mem-'ries. they're the sweet-est ones I know. Cook-ies bak-ing in the kitch-en, cards and

THE CHRISTMAS SONG
(Chestnuts Roasting on an Open Fire)

Music and Lyric by MEL TORME
and ROBERT WELLS

THE CHRISTMAS WALTZ

Words by SAMMY CAHN
Music by JULE STYNE

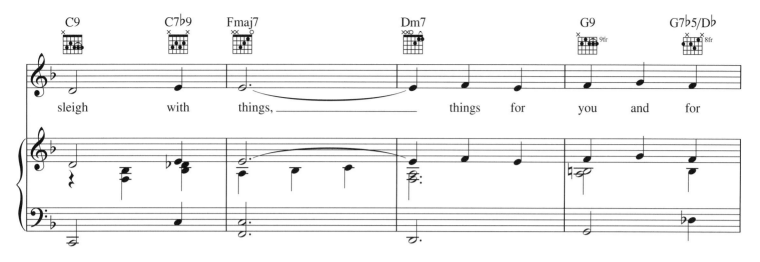

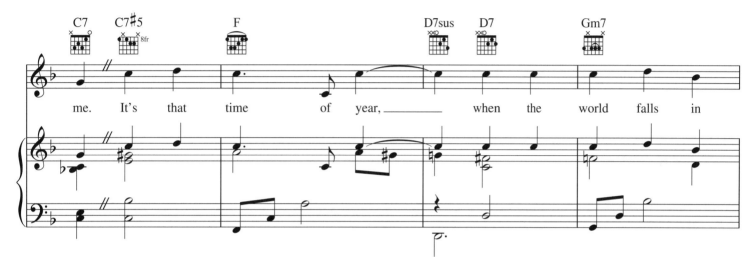

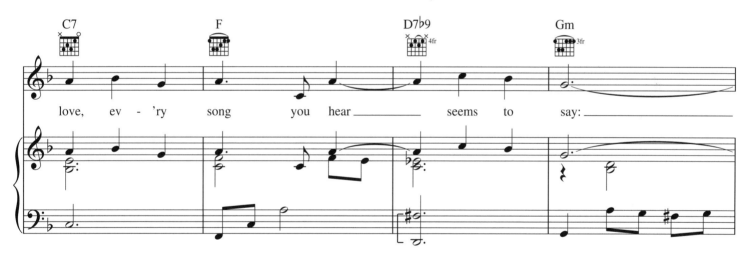

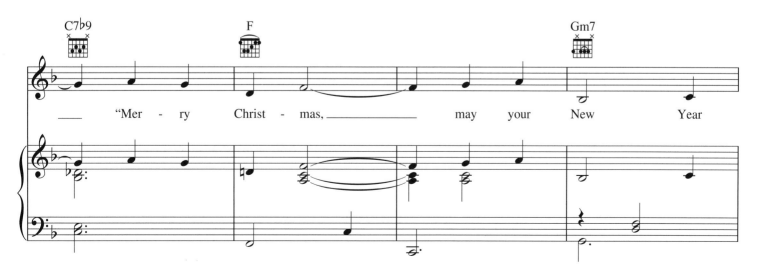

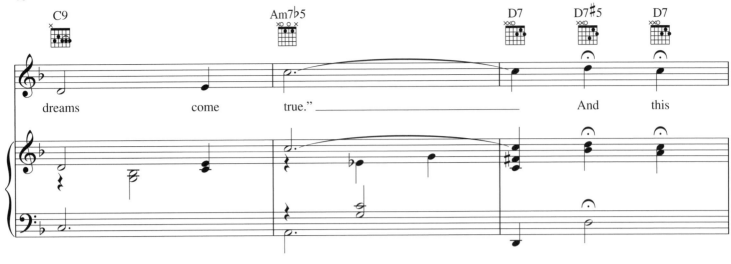

dreams come true." _____ And this

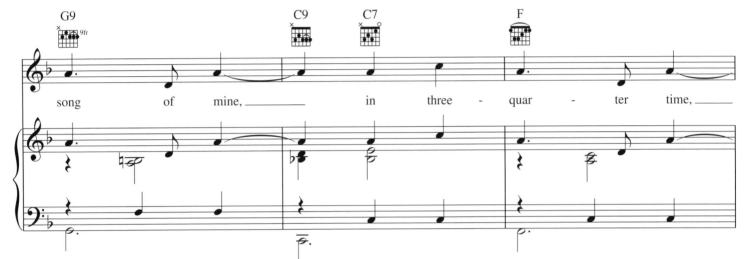

song of mine, _____ in three - quar - ter time, _____

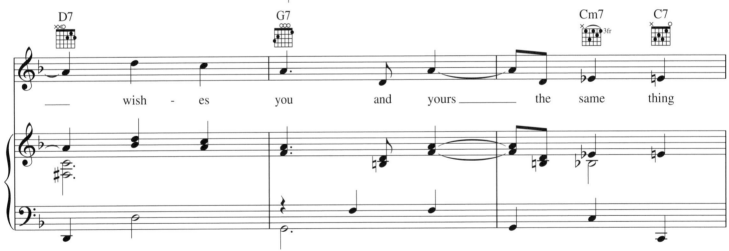

_____ wish - es you and yours _____ the same thing

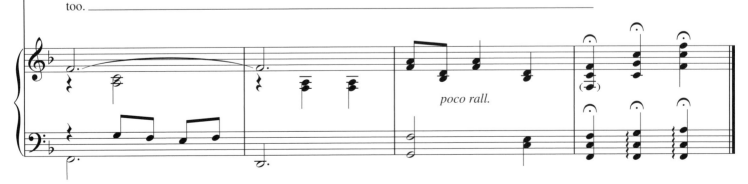

too. _____

poco rall.

I'LL BE HOME FOR CHRISTMAS

Words and Music by KIM GANNON
and WALTER KENT

12

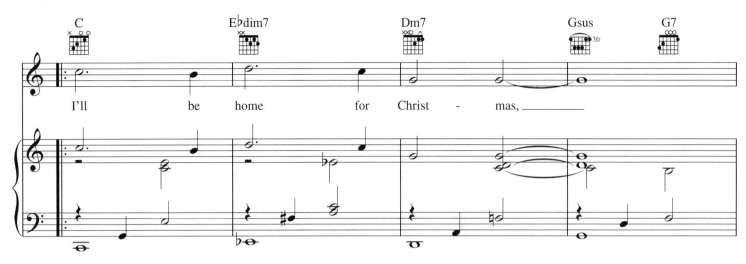

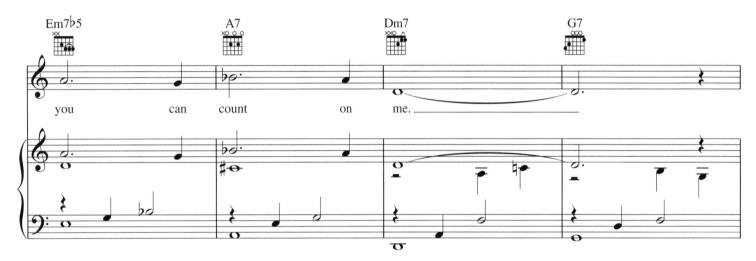

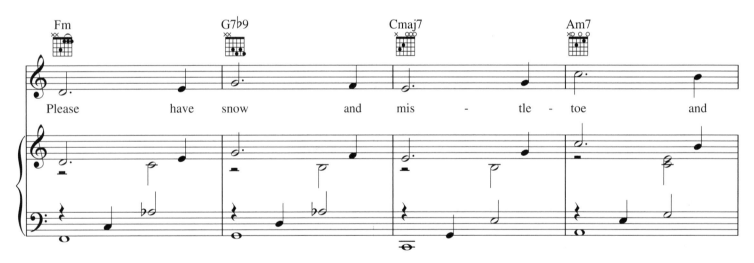

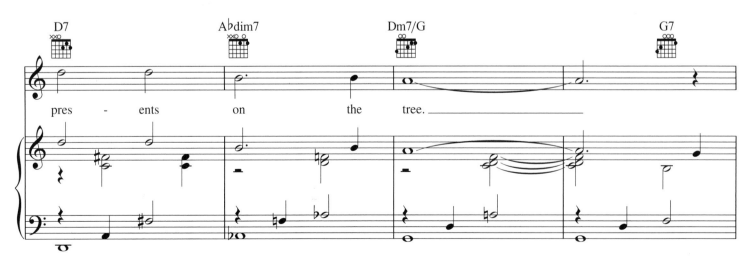

HAVE YOURSELF A MERRY LITTLE CHRISTMAS

from MEET ME IN ST. LOUIS

Words and Music by HUGH MARTIN
and RALPH BLANE

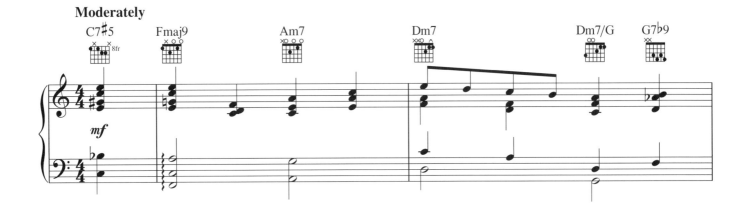

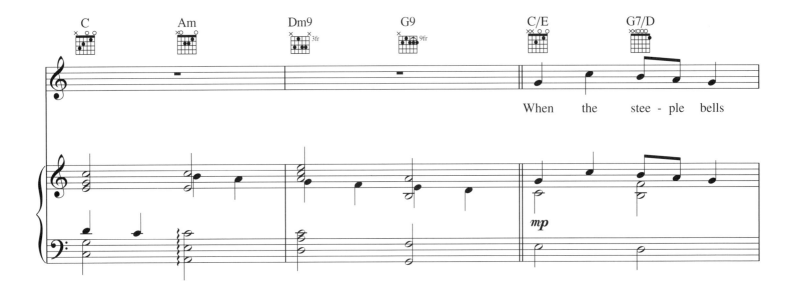

When the stee-ple bells

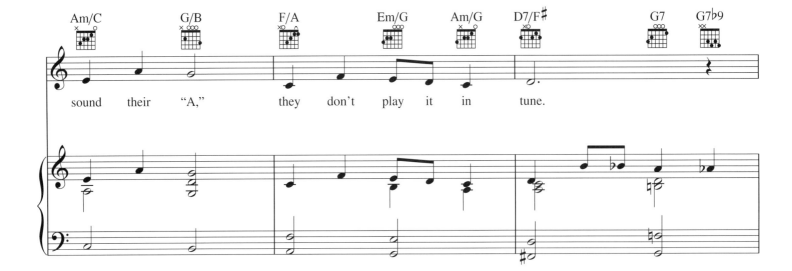

sound their "A," they don't play it in tune.

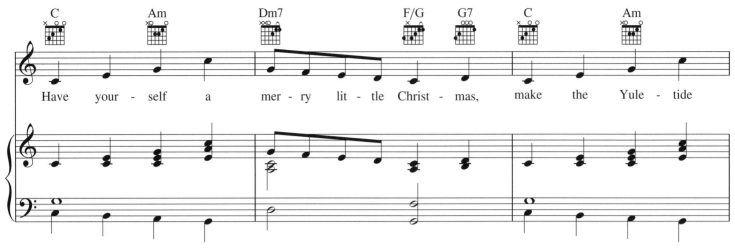

Have your- self a mer-ry lit-tle Christ-mas, make the Yule- tide

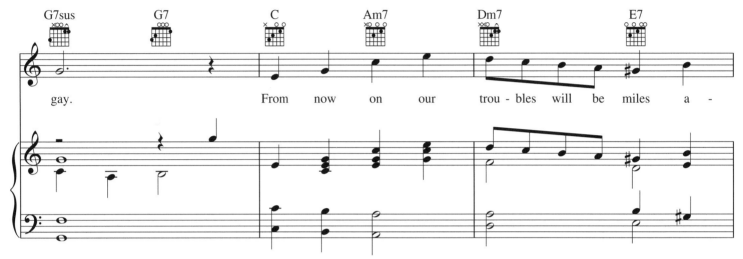

gay. From now on our trou-bles will be miles a-

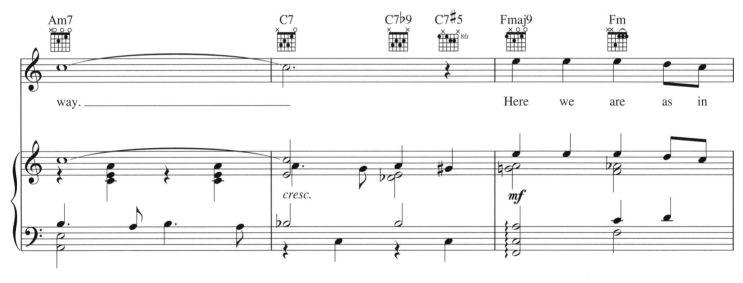

way. _____ Here we are as in

old- en days, hap- py gold- en days of yore.

have your - self a mer - ry lit - tle Christ - mas now.

Here we are as in old - en days, hap - py

gold - en days of yore. Faith - ful friends who are

dear to us gath - er near to us once more.

rit. e dim.

19

I HEARD THE BELLS ON CHRISTMAS DAY

Words by HENRY WADSWORTH LONGFELLOW
Adapted by JOHNNY MARKS
Music by JOHNNY MARKS

Moderately slow

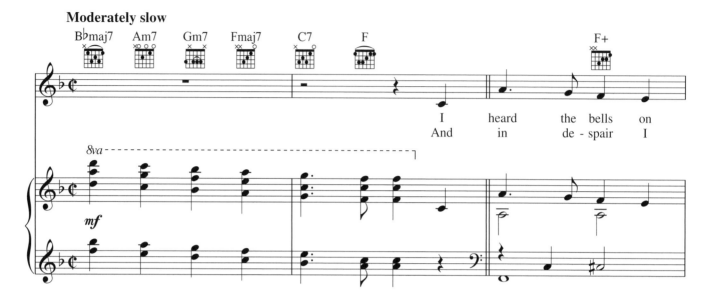

I heard the bells on
And in de-spair I

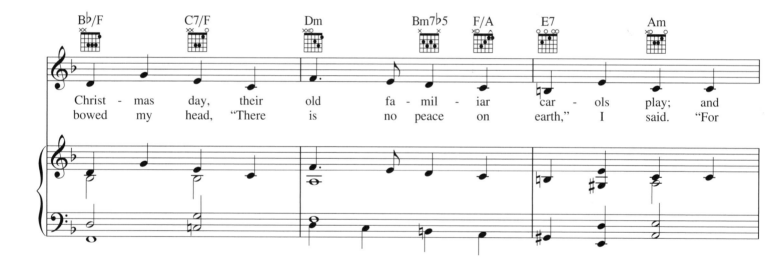

Christ-mas day, their old fa-mil-iar car-ols play; and
bowed my head, "There is no peace on earth," I said. "For

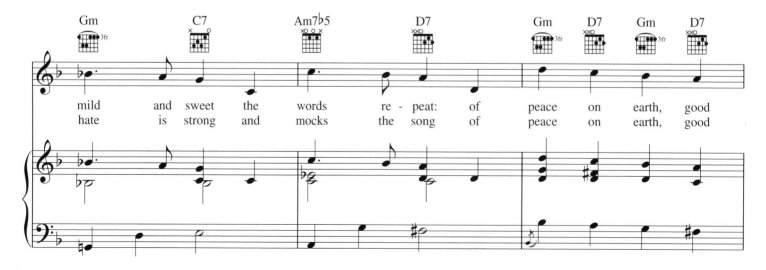

mild and sweet the words re-peat: of peace on earth, good
hate is strong and mocks the song of peace on earth, good

I'VE GOT MY LOVE TO KEEP ME WARM

from the 20th Century Fox Motion Picture ON THE AVENUE

Words and Music by
IRVING BERLIN

Bright Jump tempo

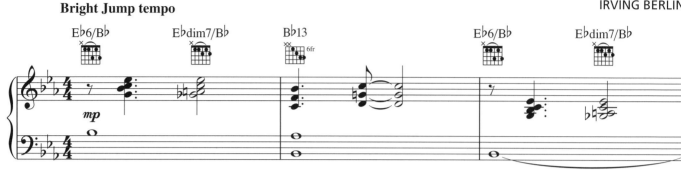

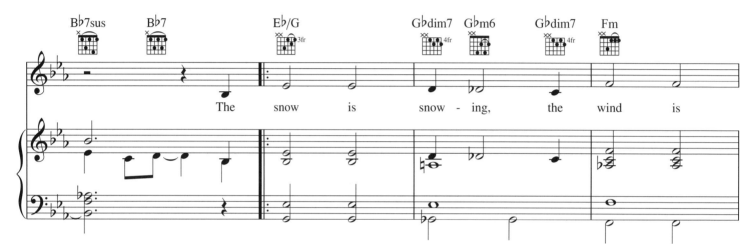

The snow is snow-ing, the wind is

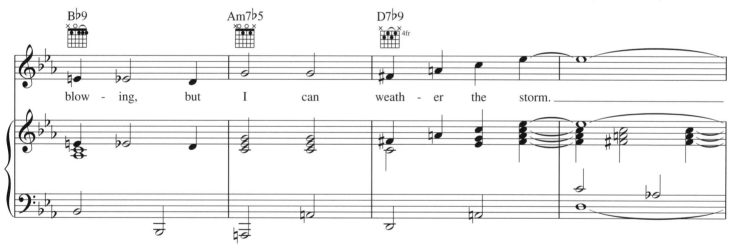

blow-ing, but I can weath-er the storm.

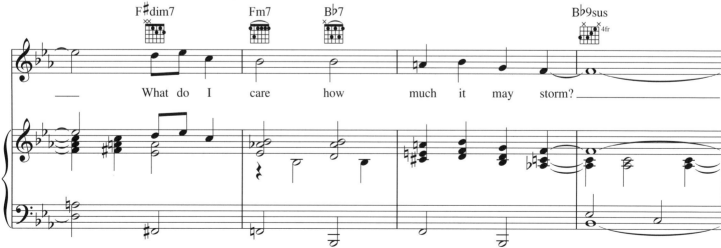

What do I care how much it may storm?

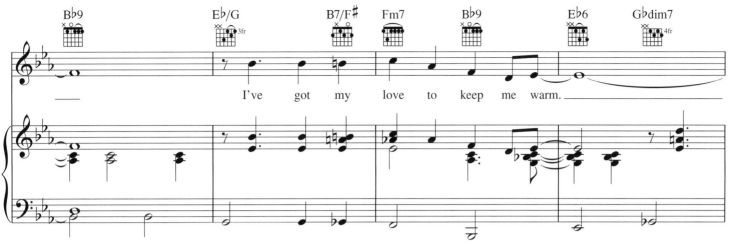

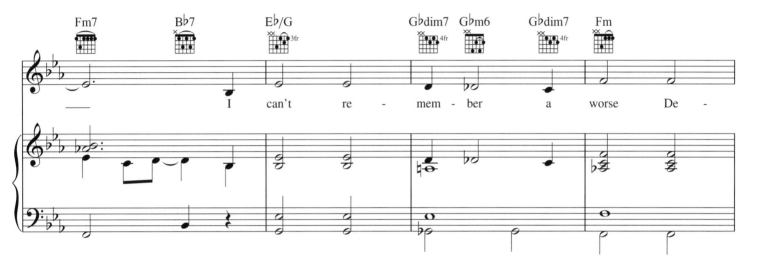

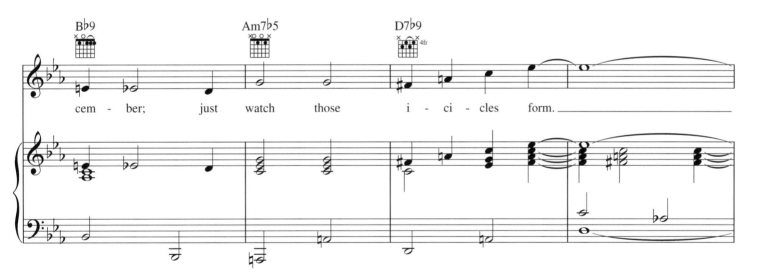

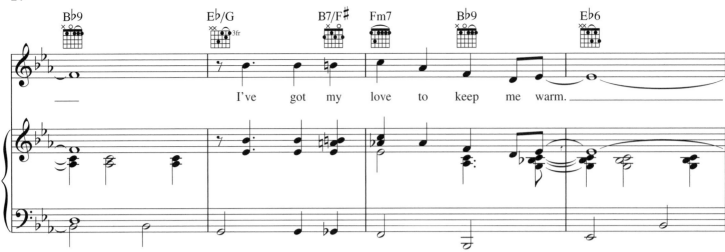

I've got my love to keep me warm. ___

Off with my o-ver-coat, ___

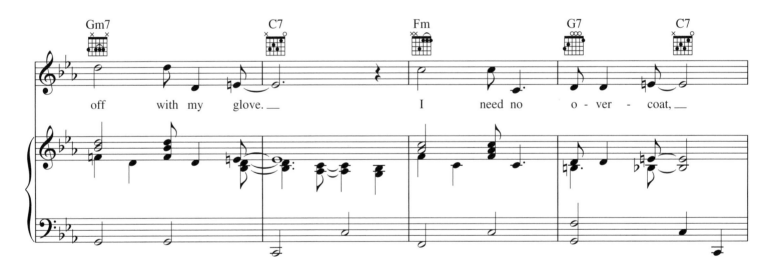

off with my glove. ___ I need no o-ver-coat, ___

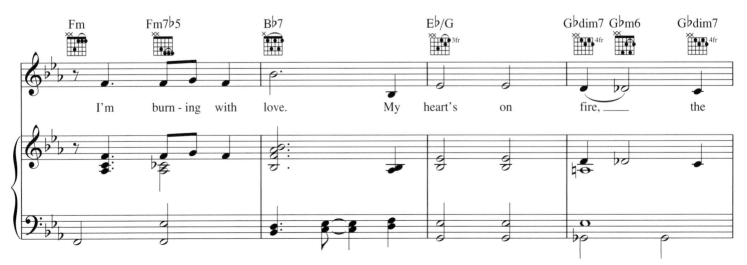

I'm burn-ing with love. My heart's on fire, ___ the

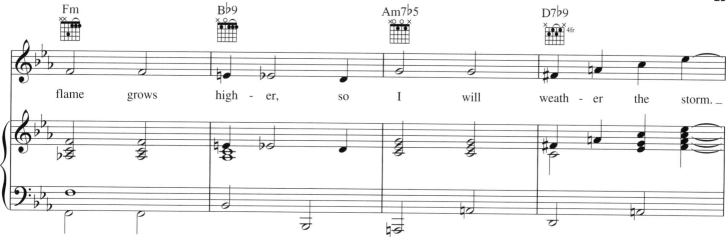

flame grows high - er, so I will weath - er the storm. _

What do I care how much it may storm? _

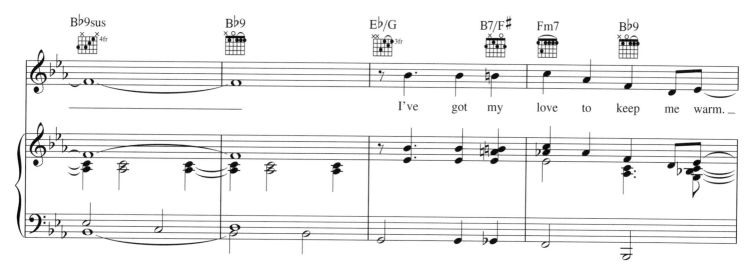

I've got my love to keep me warm. _

The

THE LORD'S PRAYER

By ALBERT H. MALOTTE

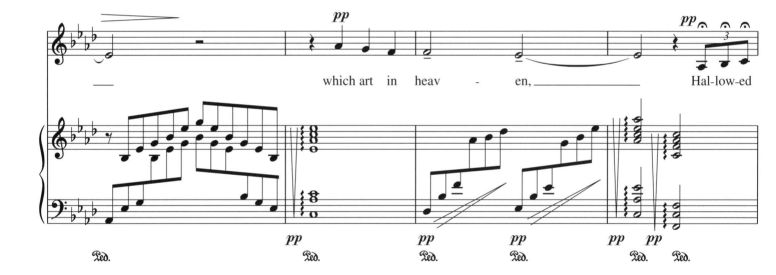

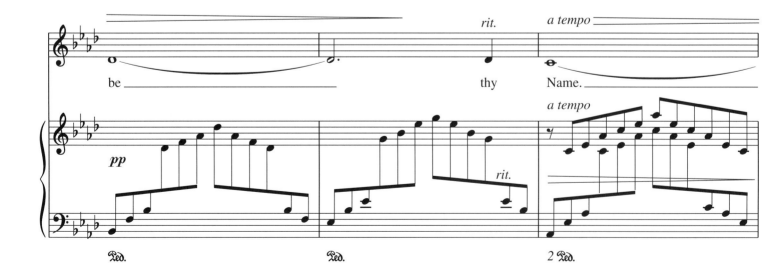

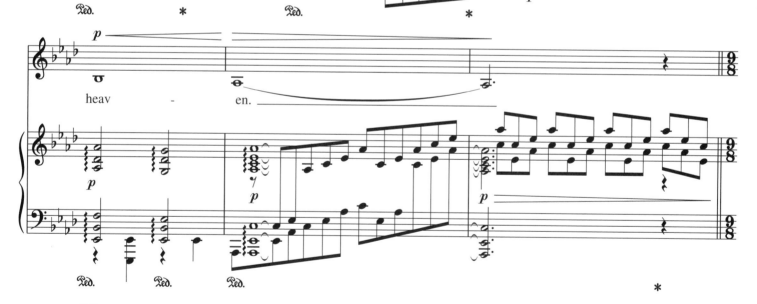

MISTLETOE AND HOLLY

Words and Music by FRANK SINATRA,
DOK STANFORD and HENRY W. SANICOLA

Oh, by gosh, by gol - ly,   it's time for mis - tle - toe and
Oh, by gosh, by jin - gle,   it's time for car - ols and Kris -
Oh, by gosh, by gol - ly,   it's time for mis - tle - toe and

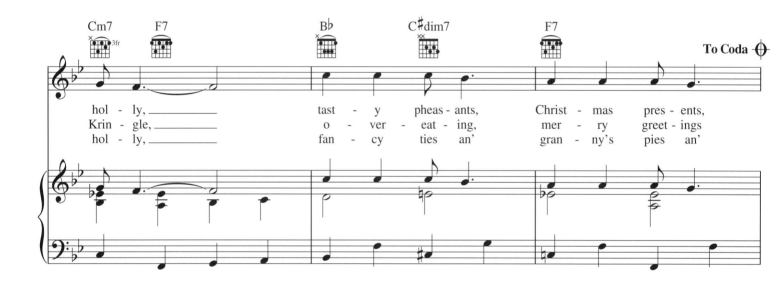

hol - ly, _____ tast - y pheas - ants, Christ - mas pres - ents,
Krin - gle, _____ o - ver - eat - ing, mer - ry greet - ings
hol - ly, _____ fan - cy ties an' gran - ny's pies an'

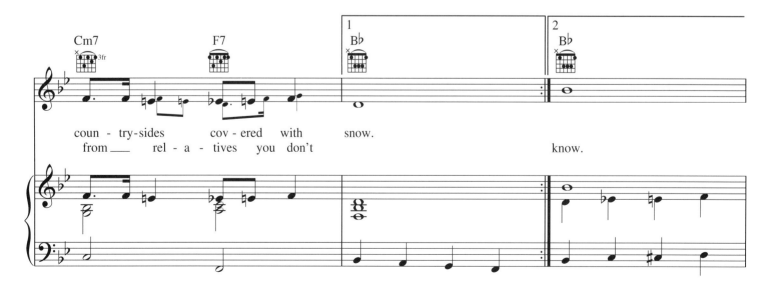

coun - try - sides cov - ered with snow.
from ___ rel - a - tives you don't   know.

Then comes that big night, _____ giv-ing the tree the trim,

D.C. al Coda

you'll hear voic-es by star-light _____ sing-ing a yule-tide hymn.

CODA

folks steal-in' a kiss or two as they whis-per, "Mer-ry

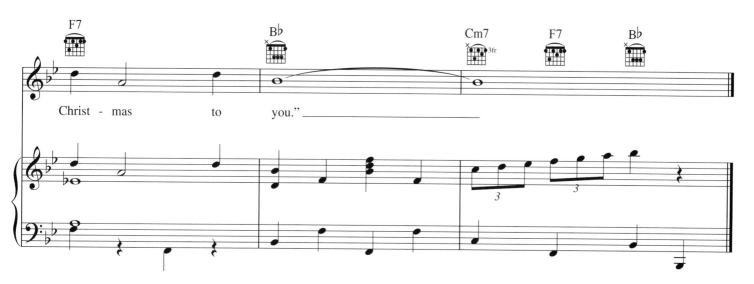

Christ-mas to you." _____

AN OLD FASHIONED CHRISTMAS

Words by SAMMY CAHN
Music by JAMES VAN HEUSEN

old fash-ioned fire-place, give me an old fash-ioned

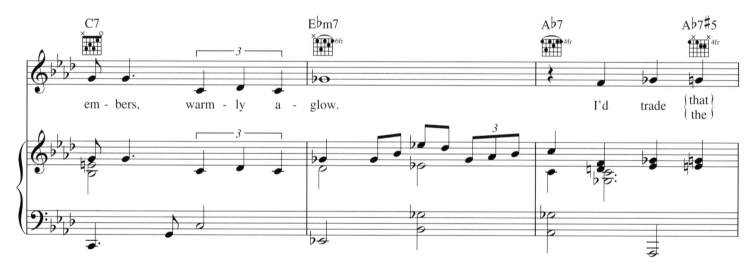

fire - place. My heart re - mem - bers smold - er - ing

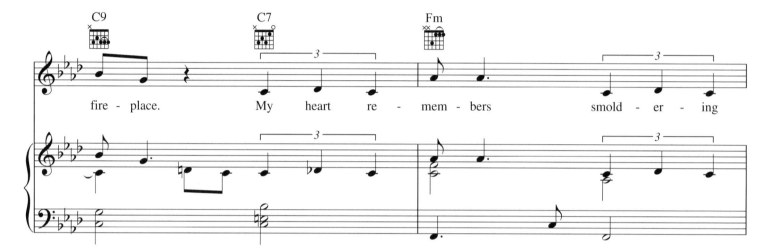

em - bers, warm - ly a - glow. I'd trade {that / the}

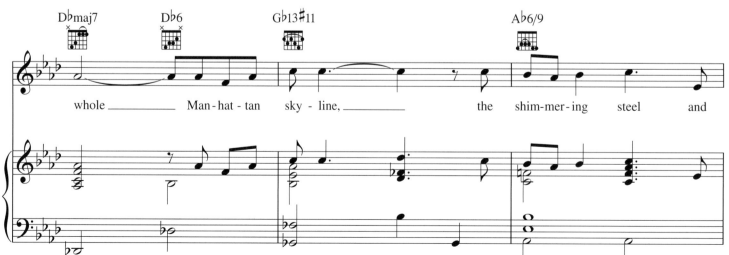

whole _____ Man - hat - tan sky - line, _____ the shim - mer - ing steel and

WE WISH YOU THE MERRIEST

Words and Music by
LES BROWN

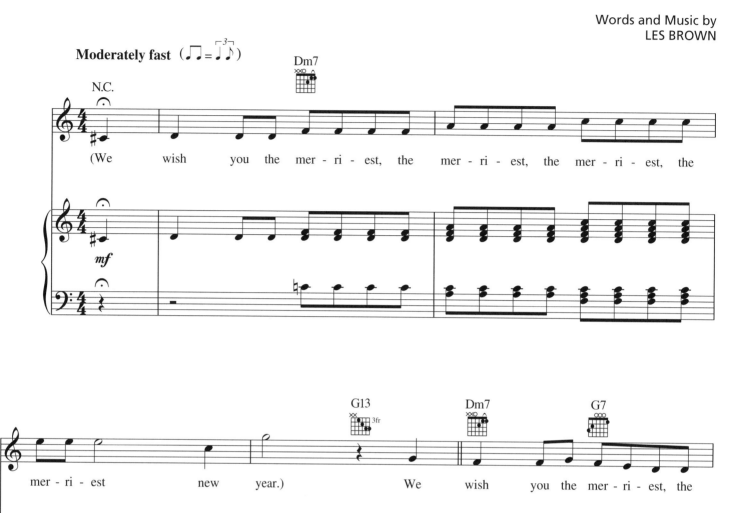

(We wish you the mer-ri-est, the mer-ri-est, the mer-ri-est, the

mer-ri-est new year.) We wish you the mer-ri-est, the

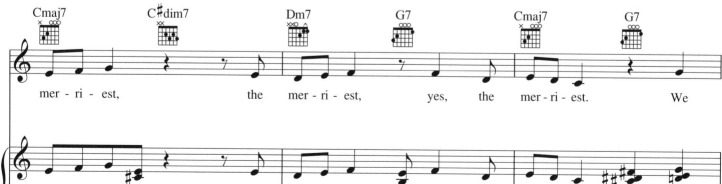

mer-ri-est, the mer-ri-est, yes, the mer-ri-est. We

wish you the mer - ri - est, the mer - ri - est the mer - ri - est yule

cheer. We wish you the hap - pi - est, the hap - pi - est, the

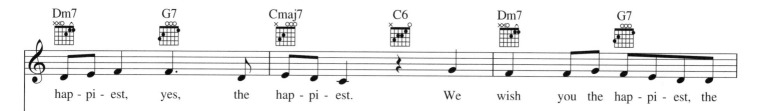

hap - pi - est, yes, the hap - pi - est. We wish you the hap - pi - est, the

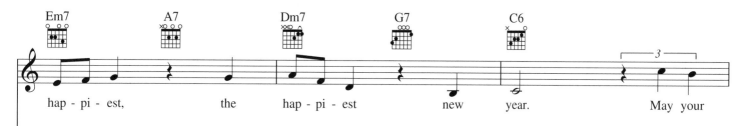

hap - pi - est, the hap - pi - est new year. May your

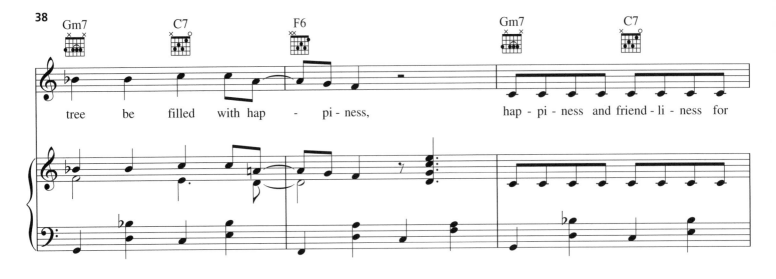

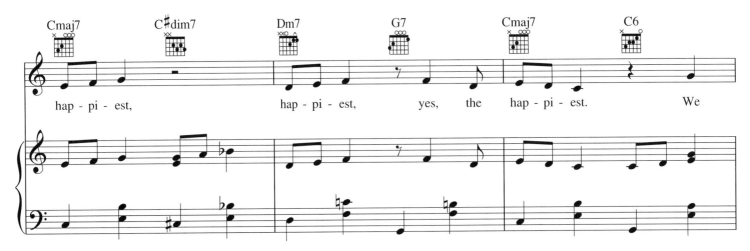

wish you the mer-ri - est, the mer-ri-est, the mer-ri - est yule

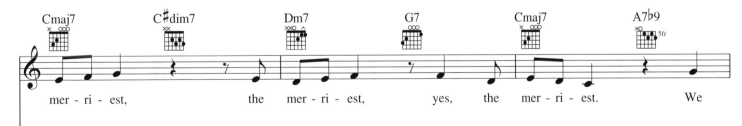

cheer and the hap-pi - est new

year. (We wish you the mer-ri - est, the

mer-ri - est, the mer-ri - est, yes, the mer-ri - est. We

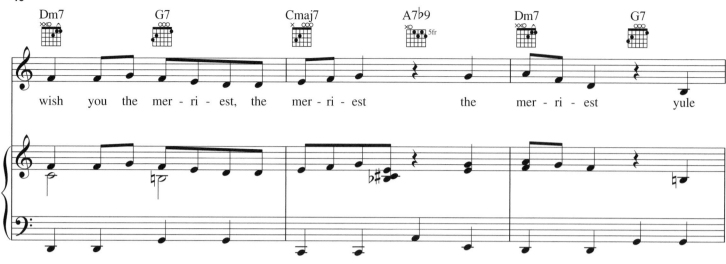

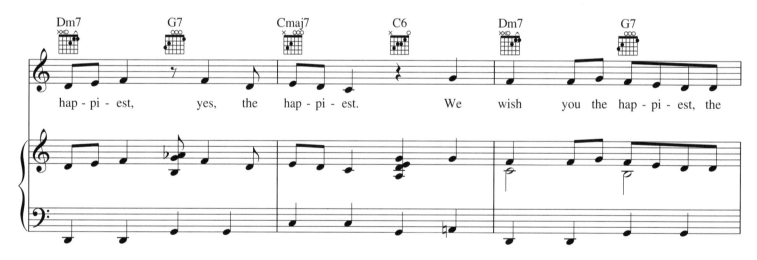

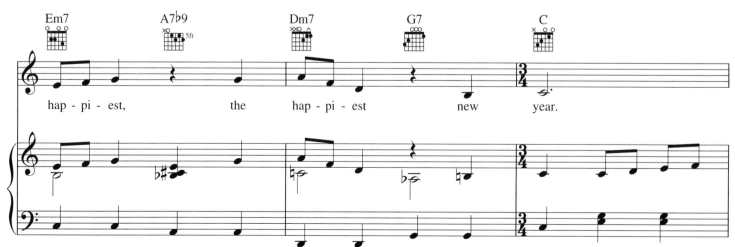

with hap - pi - ness and cheer - ful - ness and

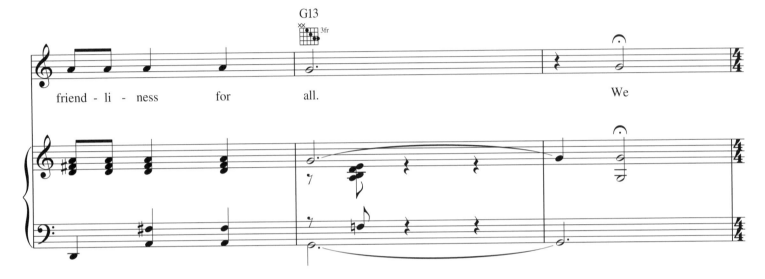

friend - li - ness for all. We

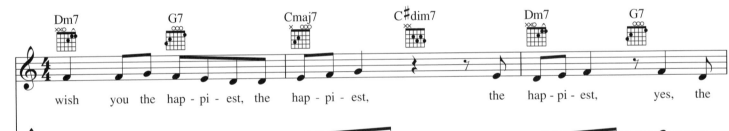

wish you the hap - pi - est, the hap - pi - est, the hap - pi - est, yes, the

hap - pi - est. We wish you the mer - ri - est, the mer - ri - est, the

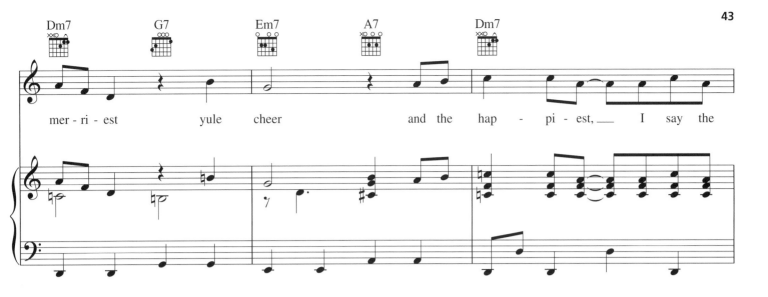

mer - ri - est   yule   cheer   and the   hap - pi - est,___   I say the

friend - li - est___ and   the   cheer - i - est,___ and e - ven   mer - ri - est   new

year._____

Slowly, forcefully

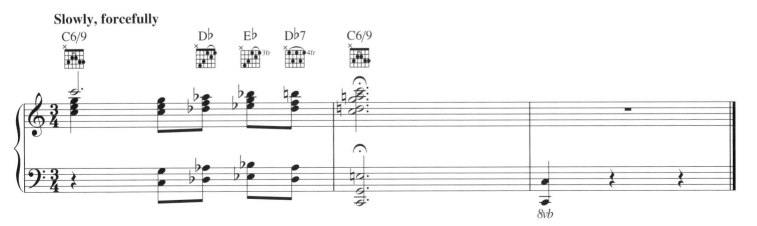

WHATEVER HAPPENED TO CHRISTMAS

Words and Music by
JIMMY WEBB

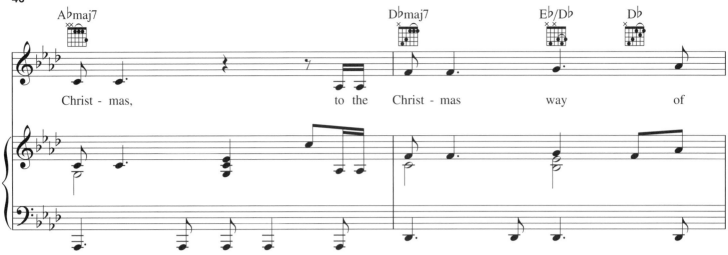

Christ - mas, to the Christ - mas way of

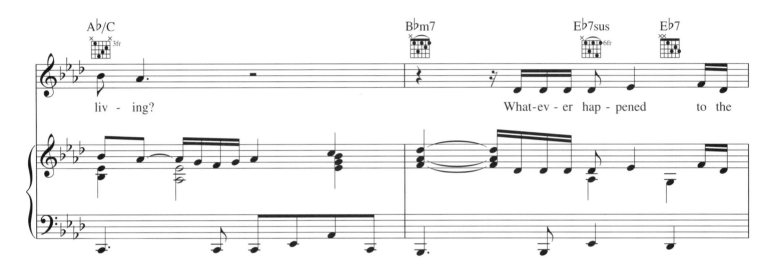

liv - ing? What-ev - er hap - pened to the

giv - ing, the mag - ic in the snow?

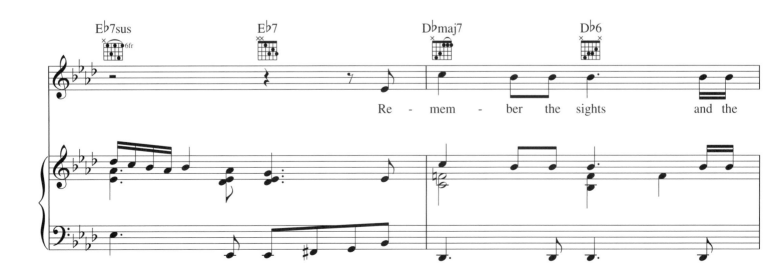

Re - mem - ber the sights and the

WHITE CHRISTMAS
from the Motion Picture Irving Berlin's HOLIDAY INN

Words and Music by
IRVING BERLIN

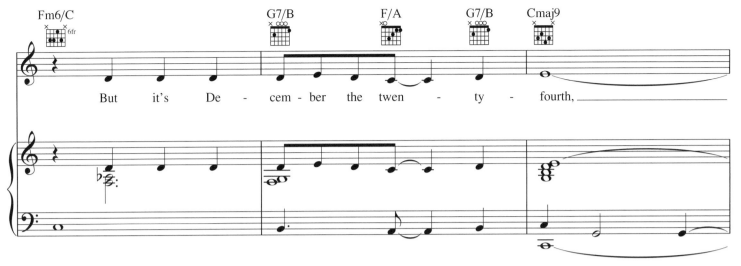

But it's De - cem - ber the twen - ty - fourth, _____

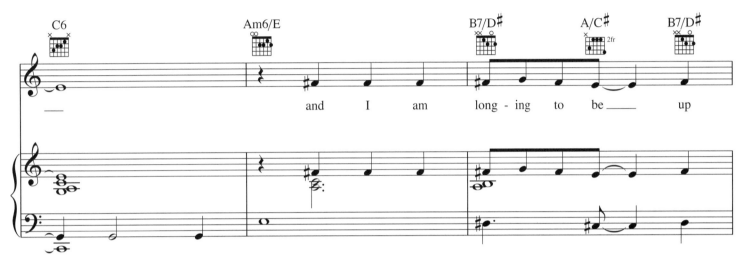

___ and I am long - ing to be _____ up

north. _____ I'm dream - ing of a

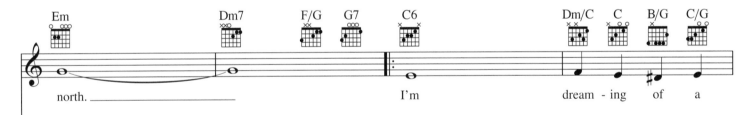

white Christ - mas, just like the

52

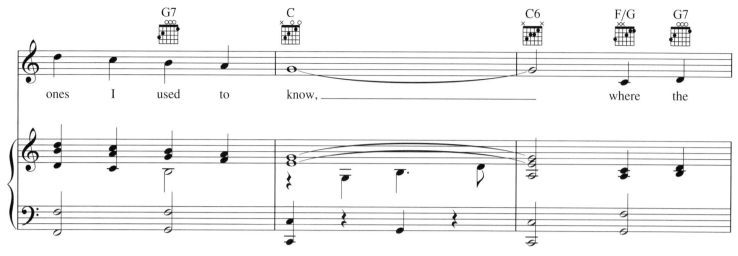

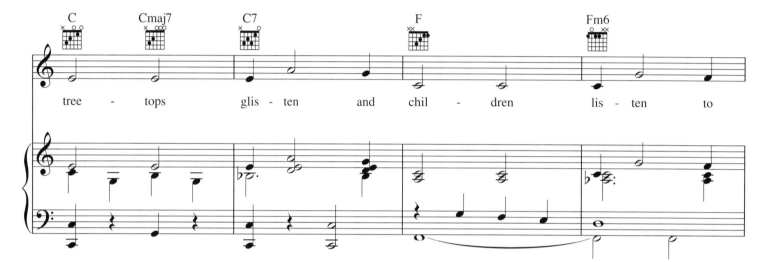

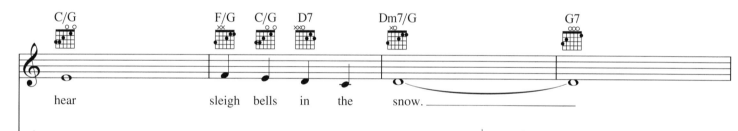

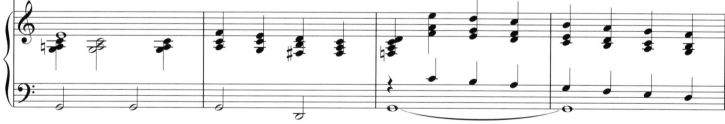

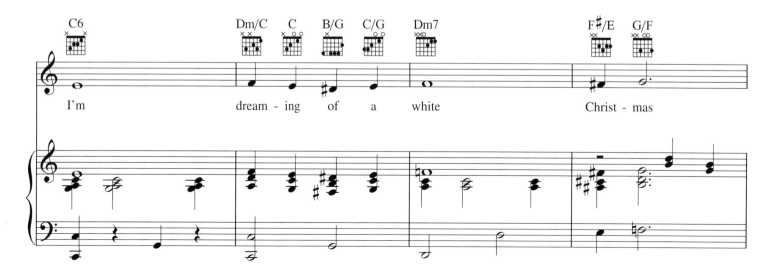

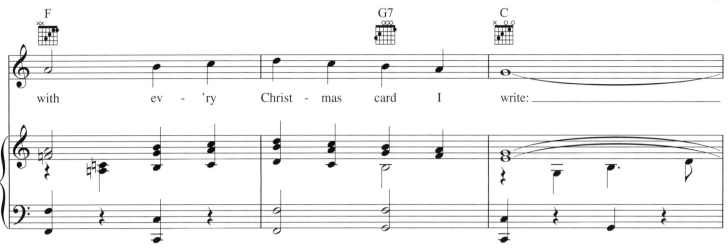

with ev - 'ry Christ - mas card I write: _____

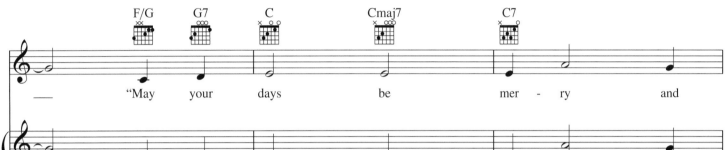

____ "May your days be mer - ry and

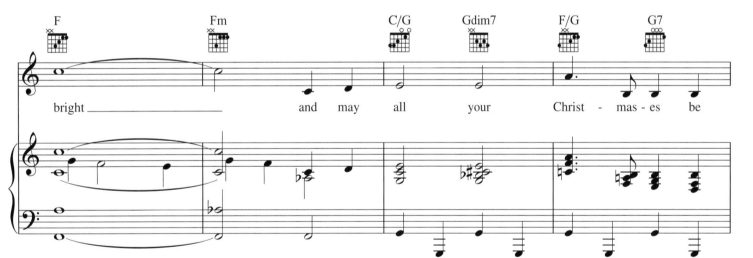

bright _____ and may all your Christ - mas - es be

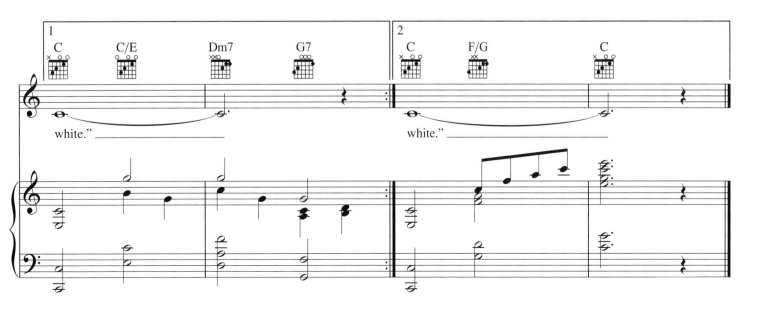

1
white." _____

2
white." _____

SANTA CLAUS IS COMIN' TO TOWN

Words by HAVEN GILLESPIE
Music by J. FRED COOTS

bad or good, so be good for good - ness sake. Oh! You

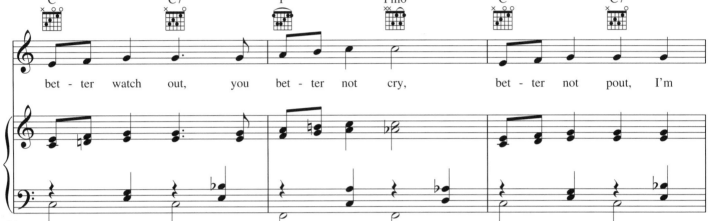

bet - ter watch out, you bet - ter not cry, bet - ter not pout, I'm

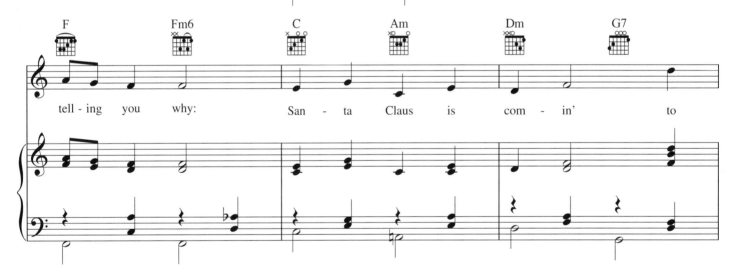

tell - ing you why: San - ta Claus is com - in' to

town. You town.